Many Ways to See the Sun

Nature Meditations for Children
and the Adults Who Love Them

B. Dierkhising (signature)

Brooke Dierkhising

Many Ways to See the Sun Copyright 2015
by Brooke Dierkhising
Illustration copyright by Brooke Dierkhising

www.manywaystoseethesun.com

Edited by Wings for Your Words
Design by Design In The Light Creative Services
Printed by BookMobile
Printed in the United States of America
on 50% PCW recycled paper

Library of Congress Cataloging-in-Publication Data
2015914626

ISBN 978-0-692-52219-6
Ebook ISBN 978-0-692-56362-5

To all children
Especially Magdalena

When children are surrounded by the simple and magnificent beauty of nature, they develop an awareness of themselves and their place in the world. They hold nature like a treasure and honor the spirit that it contains. In turn, the community also embodies this value and celebrates all life, always.

CONTENTS

*...intrinsically understand
the patterns.*

INTRODUCTION

Playing in nature allows children much-needed time to discover how things relate, change, and flow. Children build their skills: they use their minds, their bodies, and their spirits to navigate through nature's unexpectedness. They mimic the strength and resiliency. They intrinsically understand the patterns. They are endlessly wondering and in awe.

However, the reality is that often we are unable to provide long periods of free time in nature for our children. Instead, much of what is provided is planned, structured, supervised, and managed. We offer these things with all our heart, to provide safe, enriching experiences. But it is stressful. The responsibility of raising a child is a heavy one. There are so many threats, and our resources sometimes seem to shrink. And the choices sometimes are so daunting that it is a wonder we decide on anything at all. We must provide a roof over our family's heads and food on the table—and that is hard enough. And the pressure to create the perfect childhood is real and difficult to navigate. Media messages are everywhere, and it takes a lot of effort to question each one. Perhaps we suddenly waver in values which seemed so firmly in place.

We choose our life to the extent that our thinking can color our reality. So maybe it would help us to use our minds as a bridge when we can't get our kids out to play in nature as much as we would like. Children's minds are naturally gifted in the imagination department! They crave this: they must create, play, and pretend. And it might be that the more we pretend to be in nature, the more connected we become to it.

Many Ways to See the Sun is a book encouraging families to spend time with nature through story. The stories in this book are for anyone, but they are especially for children, and for the adults who care for them. Written with the child's perspective in mind, these simple guided meditations can be read out loud or silently. Read slowly and picture the narrative with your mind. Reflect on the questions that come up. The stories are arranged by the seasons. I hope you enjoy each one for the love of hearing a story, but I also hope you enjoy them more deeply. Each story is a chance to imagine, to be surrounded by nature. With each season of stories, there is also a suggested activity. These activities offer ideas for developing your connection to nature and practicing a mindfulness about your place in that relationship.

Part of the joy of being with children is that we get to relive our own childhood, in a way, through them. When else do adults get the societal OK to play in the sandbox, make funny faces, chase bubbles? So here is a tool that might make this task easier. Sit quietly with a child and imagine together; connect and have fun. Enjoy each moment you have, because, of course, it is the only one. String these special moments together to shape what is beautiful.

Feel your heart beat out
like time extending behind
you, in front of you, and now.

You Are the World

It is a warm and sunny day. The sun is shining on your face like you are the world. Our precious Earth world is over four billion years old. It sits in a universe even older. You are that universe world. Your face is a special star among many stars shining. Feel your heart beat out like time extending behind you, in front of you, and now. Wave your arms. They are like strands of seaweed. Beneath the waves they are making food from sparkles of sun. Your hands are the fins of fish swimming in the ocean. You swim to shore. Your feet walk on the sand—your delicate, strong feet. They carry you on a journey; you walk very far, and are joined by many other mammals. Your legs carry you and your blood carries the magic of that journey. The air is delicious as you breathe it in to fill your lungs. It is a new day.

You look down and see a small white ball. But it is not a ball.

Spring

Dream

It is a cool and rainy day. You watch the rain as it drops, darkening tree branches, making puddles on the ground, and sprinkling dots on your window. It looks dreamy outside and you decide to go out. You are barefoot. Feel the cold wet. Then a puddle—*brr!* The mud is cold and smooshes between your toes. You keep walking. The air is fresh and cold in your nose. Ahead, there is a row of thick bushes just beginning to bud. It stretches far on both sides. You want to see what is on the other side. What could it be? You look. There, you see a gap in the row, near the ground. You are on your knees, crawling. You are surrounded by the dark tangled branches of the bush. The ground is cold and smooth. It is quiet with just the scratching of the branches as you pass. You crawl, hand-knee, hand-knee. Then you see something bright. You realize it is the sun. You are on the other side of the bush. The rain has stopped. You crawl out of your cramped bush tunnel and stretch. You watch. *Thank you, rain. Thank you, sun. Thanks, bushes and mud.* Thank all those you remember, and also those you forget.

Tree Visit

It is a warm and sunny day. You are facing a tree. It is the most beautiful tree you have ever seen. It has invited you here for a visit. It has watched you come. The tree is looking at you and smiling. You hug the tree. Its new leaves giggle delightfully. Hear its heart beating. You lie on the ground and hold the tree's root hand. And you talk. You have a lot of things to say to each other. You look up through the bright green leaves of the tree and see the sun peeking though. The sun has joined the conversation, shimmering. You get up and you all start dancing. The sun touches your shoulder and then hops away. The tree keeps the beat by creaking its branches. You stomp around the tree. The chilly wind joins in, brushing your back. Now you are leaping after the wind. It is very fast and turns to you, thumping and drumming up your legs, on your tummy, through your hair. You twist with the wind, you grasp the tree, and then you stop, a perfect statue, the sun resting on your shoulder. You smile at the sun and the tree. You hug the tree goodbye. Walking away, you carry the visit with you inside your heart.

Garbage

It is a cool and partly cloudy day. Small patches of snow are dingy and bumpy from thawing and freezing cycles. You are on your way to see a friend. You notice the sun hiding and then peeking out of the clouds. As you walk, you see garbage: a crushed plastic bottle in the street, a candy wrapper partly tucked under snow, a chip bag crumples under your foot. You pick up a dirty plastic bag to collect all this trash. The bag is soon full. You wonder: What will happen to all the garbage I can't pick up? The melting snow will carry the trash rushing into the storm drain . . . into the river . . . will the water creatures get choked by it? Does no one else care what happens to the water, the creatures, to the Earth? Who put this trash here? Why? You begin to feel angry. Garbage is UGLY! And there is too much of it. So much waste and polluting. You finally reach your friend. Now you are crying. Your friend gives you a hug.

Hatching Egg

It is a warm and sunny day. You are walking. Misty fog covers the land like snow. But the snow is gone. You feel the soft grassy ground and the cool soft droplets on your feet. You look down and see a small white ball. But it is not a ball. You bend down to get a better look. It is a bit wet from the mist. You touch it. It is rubbery. What is that? Then! It starts to move a bit. Out pops a little brown foot. Then a head. Then another foot. Then the whole body wriggles out of the shell. It is a turtle! A baby turtle. It begins to race across the grass. Tiny blades of grass demand huge steps, but the baby is fast. How does the turtle know where to go? Following, you are a giant on tiptoes hoping not to be noticed. But this little turtle is running very fast to keep away from all danger. It is going to water. There is a marshy pond just over there. At last the turtle arrives on shore, plops into the water, and begins to paddle. You go to the edge of the marsh. You see on the other side a bunch of turtles on a log. They are piled on top of each other. Each turtle wants to be on the very top of that pile, closest to the warm sun. You see one climbing, climbing, foot on head, balancing, and oops! falls into the water. A head pops out, and the turtle begins climbing again to find a spot. Then you notice the baby turtle. She is reaching the rest of the turtles on the log. And she is home.

Duck Walk

It is a warm and sunny day. You are shopping with your family. As you cross the parking lot, you see mom and dad ducks, and behind them a row of ducklings . . . one, two, three, four, five! You gasp. What are they doing in this parking lot? Where did they come from? Where are they going? Will they be ok? There are so many cars! Your family decides to help. You all run, and then sneak near the ducks. You are almost right alongside them. You follow them. A car is near and you wave your arms in warning. The car slows, then stops. This happens again, and then again. Finally the ducks find their way across the parking lot. They cross the street too. *Whew!* No cars or people in sight. Once they are across, they are in a park. You see where they are going. There is a small lake with grasses surrounding it in the middle a small park. You stop and watch as the family of ducks waddle their way through the park. You watch as they dip and glide into the lake. The ripple goes out, out, out. You turn to your family—high fives all around!

SPRING ACTIVITY

Changes

Spring is a time of beginnings!
We leave the quiet of darkness,
and expand into the lengthening of days.
The sun's energy fuels our own.
We wake up and hear nature everywhere.

The activity for spring is about noticing change. Spring ground is frozen, then begins to thaw. Cold mud follows, and soon enough, sprouts! It is a new beginning. Then again, there is no beginning, really. Everything comes from somewhere and existed before. It has only changed and adapted to new surroundings. The cloud has no beginning, only continual change. The wind, the water, the Earth, the ground—all around us we can notice change.

And so it is within. In spring, does your heart leap? Does your heart mirror the changing seasons? Remember the last time you were standing outside and the loveliest breeze blew by, changing your mood from grumpy to smiling in a moment. Our emotions flow and pass, continually changing, like the wind. The wind is a gift.

Take a moment to notice the changes you see in nature around you. Notice your inner changes too. We go through many changes. We are strong, we are delicate, and all in between. Think of a tree, a monarch butterfly, a thunderstorm, your heart . . . strong and lasting, yet breakable too. Notice all these changes in nature and in yourself; watch them flow and continue to transform.

Weather Journal

One way to tune into change is to watch the weather. The weather is always changing, sometimes subtly and sometimes in big ways. Is there a spot you visit every day? Pick your spot, and then watch it over time. Track the weather. How and what changes in this place? Why? Record your inner feelings too. Are there similarities? Do your feelings mirror these changes? How are you transformed?

*The ground cradles you. There are
other creatures finding
shelter here too.*

Summer

Bee

It is a warm and sunny day. You are on a hilly meadow, walking. You hear the swish of the flowers as they brush your knees. The petals tickle your skin. The ground is firm under your feet. You stop and face the sun and close your eyes. The sunlight is warm on your cheeks and bright under your eyelids. You turn your head and open your eyes. In front of you, you see a tall flower, the tallest flower in the meadow, waving at you in the breeze. You go to the flower and want to smell it. Your nose is almost touching the flower when you see a bee working inside. The bee buzzes, flies to you, and lands on your nose. The bee walks around in a circle on your nose, pauses, and then flies away. It has more work to do! You see the bee zigzag and disappear.

Hello Sun

It is a warm and sunny day, just at its very beginning. You yawn, remembering how you spent the night sleeping outside under the stars. They twinkled and told you stories in your dreams. You stretch. Sitting up, you look to the east and see the sun star rising up from the line of the horizon. With it, clouds greet you, the gentlest pink and orange. You watch as the sky brightens and the colors fade to a soft blue. You are waiting and watching. The sun rises to kiss you on the forehead. *Hello, sun!* You hear a bird, and soon many birds. They all say hello too.

Whispering Rock

It is a bright and sunny day. You are hiding. Above you is a musical tree. Its round leaves are bumping out a beat. The wind sings along. You look out from your hiding place. The water is singing to you too, inviting you to join. What will you do? You like your quiet sweet song spot. You decide to come out. The ground is warm on your feet as you creep out from under the tree into the open. You walk to the water. There are rocks. The colors dazzle and entice you. You pick up a rock and hold it in your hand. What does it feel like? Notice the colors. Hold it high against the sunlight and then drop it into the water. Did you hear that? Pick it up again and put it to your heart. Listen. It has a song for you. Hear it. After some time, hug your rock and say goodbye: *I will meet you another time, my rock.* And the rock whispers back: *Thank you, my child.*

Stars

It is a warm and sunny day. It is near sunset. There are mountains in the distance. You and your family are gathering large branches. Together you first drag them and then stack them carefully. You are building a bed! There are many layers of branches. Then, you add layers of thick blankets and sleeping bags. You try it out. It is surprisingly springy and soft. One more layer on top—the humans! You all crawl into your sleeping bags. It is getting chilly and your sleeping bag is cozy. You watch as the sky changes, and then it is night. You notice yet another layer. It is above you—a blanket of stars. You are far from city lights and it is very dark, except for the stars. You see many many more than you can count. You look. Can you pick out the brightest star? Notice clusters of stars. Is that a star or a planet? Find your favorite constellation. Where is the moon? The sky is your storyteller tonight. Your eyes begin to feel heavy as your mind is filled with the stories of the stars and sky. And before you know it, you are asleep, dreaming of your own stories.

Rainbow

It is a warm and rainy day. You are walking. What is beneath your feet—the grass, the sidewalk, the sand, the mud, a log? Where are you—in the woods, your neighborhood, your backyard, a park, someplace pretend? It stops raining. The sun comes out. You are standing there. What does the wet feel like on your feet? You see the dark clouds in the distant sky and also the brightness of the sun. A rainbow! A rainbow! It arches in the sky, colors bright. Then, the colors become soft. And then, they are barely there. You lose your balance and fall back. You catch yourself on your hands. *Ouch!* You've landed on a sharp rock and cut your skin. It is a small scrape, but you are bleeding. You look around. There is a clump of plantain next to you. You ask the plant if you can pick it. *Yes*, it responds. You pick it, crumple it, and lay it over your wound. You feel the coolness as the plant begins healing your cut. The bleeding has stopped. You sit. You think of the rainbow. And think of your healing. And think of how things can both suddenly appear, and suddenly disappear.

The Wind Blows

It is a hot and humid day. Your shirt and shorts are sticking to you. You go outside in search of a swim. You walk down a path. You see a sparkling lake in the distance. You start to run. You leap into the water, creating a wave, and then you collapse in the coldness. You splash and swim for a long time. You turn and float on your back and look up at the sky. You notice the clouds are thick and the sky is turning greenish. You recognize that this is one of the many helpful signals from nature that all creatures need to find shelter from an approaching storm. You quickly get out of the water and rush back down the path. It begins to rain. The wind starts to blow, and leaves and dust are circling you. You come to a small hill, and next to it is another hill, creating a little valley in between. It is the perfect shelter. You go there and lie down. It is very windy, but you are safe. The ground cradles you. There are other creatures finding shelter here too. At your feet you can feel soft fur. A rabbit is snuggled up against the hill. It peeks at you. You peek at the rabbit. There is a whirling and whirling above your heads. It is loud, and then suddenly, it stops. The sun begins to shine again. The clouds have quickly moved on. It is cooler. You race back down the path to the lake. Now you are the tornado.

Surprise

It is a warm and partly cloudy day. You are lying in the grass looking up at the sky. You see lots of puffy shapes . . . dinosaur, ice cream cone, dog . . . what else? You turn to your side. You see something green and longish . . . a dangling chrysalis from a leaf! It is still. There is no wind, but the chrysalis begins to wiggle. You watch. You hold your breath. The chrysalis cracks and a speck of black appears. Then more! Black and orange. Soon a whole new bug appears. It is a monarch butterfly. It hangs there. And slowly, slowly, its wings grow, bigger and bigger, until they are whole and outstretched. They fan and flutter. You keep watching, very still, very quiet. You breathe slowly. And then, the butterfly flies! You watch, you clap. You get up from the grass, following the butterfly, clapping and cheering. *Happy metamorphosis, beautiful one!*

Sand and Toes

It is a hot and sunny day. Your toes are sinking into the soft sand. They are getting colder as you dig down with your big toes and then . . . kick! The sand goes flying, spraying your shoulders and into the space around you, like shimmering stars. Each little grain of sand is like a star in the universe. Each grain of sand is the universe, but so tiny. You leap your whole body into the air. You race to the water, your feet thumping on the soft sand. Stomp, stomp, stomp, and splash! The water is cold. You swim and the water carries you like a soft pillow. Swim, swim, swim, and stop. You are still. You stand in the water and dig your toes into the sandy bottom. You have planted yourself. Nature begins to visit. First a leaf floats by, carrying some sunlight. Then a few fish look at your legs, a mystery to them (you are not food!) and swim on. As you turn to shore, a dragonfly lands on your wrist. You lift it, and you are face to face. What are you both thinking? It winks and flies away. You wave. And then you hide, under the water, just for a moment. You swim back to shore, and step by step, soft sand and toes.

SUMMER ACTIVITY

Wonder

*Summer is lightness. We worship the sun.
The world bursts with color and smells.
We play, we sweat, we splash,
and joy is everywhere . . . in the flowers,
the rivers, the insects, the clouds.
We join in the fun.*

The activity for summer is simple and wondrous reverence. The days are longer and we have more light. Shadows are a contrast, a mystery among the celebration. We make time to enjoy, relax, and have fun—to be social with family and friends outside in nature. We are seduced by the light; it brings us such joy, and we play. We are in the present moment and connect with the living world. We are graced with this lightness. We release and are filled. Every thought, every word, every action is a joyful prayer. We give reverence to the wonders of summer.

Plant Visiting

Bring out the magic of summer by planting a garden. Maybe it is a tiny garden—a flower in a pot, or a huge one—many varieties of vegetables on acres of land, or anywhere in between.

Grow something!

Choose a favorite plant. Prepare the soil, plant the seed, water it, and tend to it. Watch it sprout and grow.

Talk to your plant. Pray for it. Pray for all the plants on Earth. Welcome in the little critters with honor—butterflies, ants, birds, bees, worms. Watch them care for other living things—and be nourished.

Visit your garden, tiny or huge or in between, every day, and open yourself to the immense wonder of this complex system and simple beauty.

The wind blows and the falling leaves rustle past your feet, twisting around your legs.

Fall

Leaf

It is a cool and breezy day. The leaves dance on the ground, playing with the wind. You want to play too. You kick up the leaves as you walk. What a loud rustling they make as you swish and stomp through. They whirl, whirl around your feet. The piles invite you. You bend down to scoop up a bunch. So bright, so yellow. *Fly up, leaves!* They rain down on you, and you twirl with them. More, more scooping . . . and fly up . . . and twirl. You jump, you stomp, you scoop, you toss, playing with the leaves. And then you fall in a big heap. What a soft pillow for your whole body. You rest, looking up at the sky. How blue it is. And how yellow the leaves are, slowly falling down. You watch as one leaf twists and turns, falling and falling, and then lands right near your heart. Hold the leaf in your hand and admire the color, the lines, the shape. This is a gift for you.

Squirrel Party

It is a warm and sunny day. You are watching a squirrel. It is sitting on top of a pumpkin, sharp-clawed paws holding a piece and nibbling, tail curled and twitching. The squirrel finishes the last bite, looks around, and goes bounding for a tree, up, up. There is another squirrel going down, down. They begin to chase each other, around and around the tree. Then a leap and they go their separate ways. Several squirrels scurry around on the ground and in the trees. They are busy! Burying nuts, darting, dodging, so quick . . . leaping, chasing, looking, finding . . . then sitting for a moment. Break open a nut and eat the delicious meat inside. All the squirrels are doing this. It is a squirrel party. And you like to party too.

Puppy

It is a cool and sunny day. You are going for a walk before dinner. It is almost sunset. You keep walking. The path is easy—a forest floor, dirt mostly. The trees stretch above you, tall ferns to the side tickle your legs sometimes as you go. It is still. You keep walking. After a while you reach the forest edge. There is a steep slope leading down to a river. You look way down, and across. You notice the difference of this open space compared to the closed forest pathway behind you. *Oh! A puppy!* It jumps on your leg. You bend down to pet it and it licks your hand. A child is following the puppy. You both say hi and introduce yourselves. Then the child asks you if you would like to play at their family campsite. *Fun.* So you go with the child and puppy just around the bend. You sit by the fire, watching it flicker, orange and yellow. You hear this family talk and laugh. You have a joke to tell too. You stay for a bit, but then say your goodbyes and head back down the forest path. As you arrive at your own forest home, your family greets you. Dinner is just being set on the picnic table. You sit down and see next to you that the puppy has followed you. You sneak a treat and feed it to the puppy. The puppy turns and heads back home, tail wagging.

Sunflower

It is a chilly and sunny day. What a commotion! You hear birds chirping like it is a bird music festival. You peek outside your window to see. Brown birds, yellow birds, blue birds, black birds . . . they are all flying, looping, and landing on the sunflowers. It is a field of sunflowers right in your own backyard. The birds are having a harvest party! They know when the seeds are ready to eat . . . they smell them, they see them, and they know. They eat them! The seeds are oh so yummy and delicious as they snap open the shell and the rich and tender seed bursts with flavor. The birds sing, they eat, and they dance with each other, over and over, so happy for the fall feast. You watch, and you want some sunflower seeds too, but you stay your distance. You honor their place as first. You will have your sunflower seeds, perhaps tomorrow, when it is your turn, and if there are any left! You watch the dancing, chatting, eating birds a bit longer. And then you turn and walk to go back inside, the warmth of the sun on your back.

Spooky

It is a cool and windy day. You are walking home. The shadows from the setting sun are getting longer. The sky is orange behind the dark, blackened trees. The wind blows and the falling leaves rustle past your feet, twisting around your legs. Someone screams, then laughs. They are playing somewhere far off. A cat seems to be following you. You hear footsteps and someone runs past you. The squirrels hurry from tree to tree. It is getting darker. You begin to walk more quickly. You have just a bit farther to go. Then you see your home. It is dark. Is no one home? You stop to search for your key in your bag. Where is it? You feel a tickling on your hand. A spider! You jump. The spider releases its silk, dangling to the ground until it is free from you. You've dropped your bag. Is there another spider in my bag, you wonder? You stare at it. The bag seems to stare back. Deep breath. You quickly open the flap. Nothing. You look inside. Nothing. You carefully search for your keys again. There, you've got them. You grab your bag and head to your door. It is still dark inside. You slowly open the door with a creak . . . *BOOOOOO!* The lights turn on and your family giggles. They scared you good!

Bird Message

It is a cool and breezy day. You are wearing a hat. Your hands are in your pockets. You are walking along a path. The leaves crunch under your feet. You look up. The tree branches are bare and seem dark against the pale sky. You keep walking and walking. Notice the sounds all around you: the breeze whispers past; your footsteps softly thud on the ground; there is a tiny sound of an animal scurrying; the trees creak gently. And then, the wind gusts like a message. You stop. A pile of leaves swirl, and underneath, lying on the ground, is a small red bird. You go to it and it blinks at you. It is scared of you and tries to move its wings, but it is tangled in something wiry. You sing a lullaby to the bird. You begin to gently peel away the tangles. Once it is free, the bird lies there for a moment, looking at you. Then it begins to sing to you. It hops and stops to ruffle a bit, then uses its beak to smooth its feathers. It looks at you once more, then flies way up up up to a tree . . . then swoops down and away out of sight. You touch your heart with your hand and wave goodbye. You continue walking, whistling softly to the forest, telling all that you are a friend.

FALL ACTIVITY

Gratitude

A finale of such bounty,
and with an explosion of intense beauty,
we surrender to the end. It is fall.
The sun shines less brightly,
and we hurry to enjoy the abundance.

The activity for fall is to notice our blessings. We receive so much; it is necessary to be grateful. All we are is because of what came before us. Listen to the voices of your ancestors and acknowledge these special gifts. Consider your immediate past as well as your deep past. See all your family around you, those related by blood and those related by the heart.

I am in awe of the bounty of blessings given to me both today and from extending time past. Like my grandmother's laughter running through my blood, my

DNA. Her gifts are part of me . . . her laugh, her swift card playing, her applesauce, her cookie perfection, her grapevines, her organizational finesse, her practical quilt stitch, and so much more. We all have these memories, this special bounty, this supreme support. Our ancestors offer us a never-ending river of gifts.

Ancestral Tree

Consider the stories of an ancient tree. We often use the branches of a tree to represent how the individuals in a family are related. The tree grows as our families grow. The root system is as vast as our ancestral history.

1. Draw a tree including the roots.
2. Who came before you? These are the roots.
3. Who is your family now? This is the trunk.
4. What gifts have they bestowed? These are the branches.
5. How do you use/honor these gifts? These are the leaves?
6. How do you give thanks? This is the air and soil.

*You see the sun shining on the snow
and it glistens.*

Winter

Hoot

It is a cold and cloudy day. It is only late afternoon, but it is almost dark. You get bundled up and go outside. You march out the door, take a few steps, and hoot out into your yard. Hoot! Hoot! Footprints, snow tunnel, fallen branches, squirrel nest, milkweed pods, icicles. This is your world today, shared by all, belonging to anyone. This yard is a place of peace. Now it is snowing . . . you catch snowflakes on your tongue. Your head weaves after them. Your cheeks turn cold. The sky turns dark. The moon appears. The moon is so bright; its light reflects off the snow.   You take a few steps. You stand still. It is so quiet. You hear only your breath, and if you listen carefully, the snow falling to the ground and on you.

Crows

It is a cold and sunny day. Everywhere you look it is white. The ground is white and glistening with sunshine sparkles. The trees are layered, dark and white. You are walking along a wide path. All around you is quiet, still, white. A flock of black birds fly overhead, calling: Caw! Caw! They land at the very top of the very tallest tree. Crows, black against the bluest sky. They are talkative and social. You listen and you watch. You want to talk too: Caw! Caw! They are still now and watching you. And then . . . Caw, caw! You run, arms out, footprints marking the snow, rushing down the path. Caw, caw! Your feet are pounding and there is such a noise in the trees now. The crows are all flying with you, many, many, black, black, black. Together you fly. Fly! Crows flying up and up and up . . . until they are only dots against the blue sky. Caw! Caw! Caw! Caw! they exclaim. You stop, and your spirit continues to fly up with them. Your heart is full of the cawing sound. You are with them, and you are alone with the quiet snow.

Gloomy

It is a bright and sunny day. But it feels like a dark cloud is following you wherever you go; you are feeling gloomy. So even though the sun is shining, you are not smiling. You put on your many layers of warmth and drag yourself out of the house. Your boots are like rocks as you walk to your favorite tree. Poor tree. The wind broke a branch in the storm last night. You hug your tree. You sit down and take a good look at the broken branch. It is dark except for the white ends where it was broken. You feel lonely. Blue sky. You are tired and sad and bored. You lie down under your tree. The snow is like a soft bed. You feel an icy breeze cross your face. The sun shines on you. You take a breath, a breath, a breath. You sense the warm glow of your heart. Looking around you, you belong. This is your place, and it wraps you in an invisible hug. You feel that hug. And you are held by the Earth and loved.

Winter Melt

It is a cold and sunny day. You are bundled up and walking. The ground and trees are covered with magical frost. You walk very far. Now the frost has gone and it starts to turn warm. It is turning into one of those winter thaw days. You unzip. The air rushes into your jacket. You don't need a scarf now. You unravel it from your neck and it dangles to your legs. You continue to walk. Now you take off your hat, and even your mittens! You stuff your pockets with these extras. You pick up treasure for your pockets too: a pine cone, a broken walnut, a stick. All around the melt is crackling. You see the sun shining on the snow and it glistens. Icicles are drip, dripping. It is so bright you have to squint your eyes. You watch your feet as you continue to walk, tiny brown patches of earth revealed as you go. The air is so fresh. The smell fills your nose, and you can't help breathing more and more of it. You can't get enough of this hopeful day.

Wheee, That Was Fun

(written by Magdalena, age 8)

It is a warm but brisk evening. And you are about to go on an adventure. You get on your snow pants, your coat, and also your gloves, mittens, and hat. Then you are ready for the adventure. You go outside and you see where you want to go. Finally you see a faraway bush. You run to it as fast as you possibly can. Then once you get there you go through the bare branches and you climb the tree. You grab a branch, you sit on it, and then you grab another branch. You pretend you are climbing the branch, but the branch is way too steep to climb, so you cannot do it. Then you decide to slide down the branch. Wheeee. It's fun. So you do it again. Finally you start getting bored of it, so you decide to run around the yard a few times. Then you get tired of running around the yard, and it is getting dark outside. So you decide to go inside and have a nice cup of hot chocolate. As your mom greets you at the door, you say, That was fun, and some day I will do it again.

Circle of Air

It is a cool and sunny day. You are outside at your favorite place. Look around you. Turning slowly, draw a circle around you as far as you can see. What do you see? Notice what parts of nature you can name. Notice what you cannot name. Smell the richness around you. Do the smells match what you see? Listen. What do you hear? What is the tiniest sound? Sit down and touch the ground; feel its strength as it supports you. Imagine the smallest organism under the frozen ground. What is happening below? Now look to the sky. What is above? Consider what you do not see there— the molecules in the air moving with the wind, bouncing from place to place, disappearing and reappearing. Feel your breath as part of this air. Put your hand on your heart. Breathe and pause. Stretch out your arms and give your love to this circle, and beyond. Notice the love coming back to you.

WINTER ACTIVITY

Reflection

With the darkness of winter we find stillness.
We rest and draw inward. As the sun reflects
on the snow, so does the heart.
But there is a tension; we are restless too.

We turn inward in winter, following the natural rhythm of hibernation. Our bodies crave rest and we enjoy the comfort of warm foods, a cozy fire, and a good book. A story can light up these darker days to keep us in the present moment. Or it can help us transcend time. A story sparks our creativity and activates our imagination, entertaining while teaching. Reflecting on our personal experiences, we create our own stories—and reveal life as profound.

Storytelling

Stories are everywhere. There are very old ones, and new. Some have a formula and some have tragic twists or surprises that delight us. Some are simple, some complex. You may have noticed that the stories in this book have a persistent pattern. Try this formula to create your own nature story:

1) Set the story in the present, beginning with the line: It was a warm and sunny day (or cold and cloudy— whatever suits your setting).

2) Begin describing what you might see on that particular day. Use all your senses to create the experience of your story.

3) Next, add an action. It could be as simple as going for a walk.

4) After you have settled on your scene and beginning actions, create a conflict to be solved or a happening that plays out. This is where you can stretch your imagination. Or, simply describe one of the amazing encounters you have experienced in nature!

5) End the nature story by solving your problem or winding down your described experience. And then finish with a final emotional thought—perhaps one of gratitude or wonder or safety.

6) Share your story! Or if you prefer, tuck it away to read to yourself another time.

We will heal together.

AN INVITATION

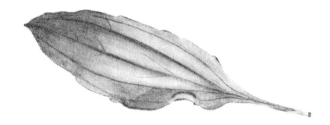

Take a moment to close your eyes and remember a special place in nature that you loved as a child. What did it look like? How did it feel? What did you do there? Were there distinct smells? What was the light like? Were you alone? Or was someone with you? Have you ever gone back as an adult?

I long for nature in my life today. As an adult with a predictably busy life, I cherish those moments when time stands still. Nature does that for me. I am amazed by the beauty of a tree, a vast canyon, crashing waves, the tiniest rock, the song of a bird, and how in August I look up to the sunflowers in my backyard against the blue of the sky and am in awe. They sway in the breeze. Some fall over from their own heaviness. The bees tend to them, in any case. Nature is happening all around us. In the country, city, down the highway, in our backyards, along the forest path, flowing in water, everywhere . . . especially in our hearts.

If we listen to our hearts, we can hear nature calling us to be part of it. It asks us to join in.

On our Earth there is much devastation. And there is much beauty. We can see both worlds. We must see both. I encourage you to embrace the beauty, express gratitude, and give reverence to the Earth we share today. We will heal together.

Take your child's hand and go into nature. Feel the breeze, notice the sparkling light, be with nature! Bless the spaces you love. Write about them. Create art. Talk about them. Dream about them. Think about them with both your mind and your heart. Share in the beauty that is here for us now.

What special place will you discover next?

ABOUT THE AUTHOR

Brooke Dierkhising has drawn inspiration through numerous wonder-filled experiences with children in nature, and through the tremendous care witnessed by the adults who tend to them. She has a Master in Education from Northwestern University and several years experience leading and creating enrichment programming for children. She finds joy in being a teacher, a mother, drawing, singing, puppetry, her toes in the mud, and spending as much time as possible contemplating the wind and sparkling trees. Brooke lives in Minneapolis with her family. This is her first book.

www.manywaystoseethesun.com

MY WARMEST THANKS
TO THE CHILDREN AND
FAMILIES OF KIDS CLUB
AND TO THE MANY OTHERS
WHO MADE THIS BOOK POSSIBLE